How to Hypnotize Your Grandchildren

Also by George Toth, LCSW-R

Marble Mindfulness: Unlock Your Family's Hidden Messages

How to Hypnotize Your Grandchildren

Easy, Quick, and Fun Ways to Influence the Children in Your Life

George Toth, LCSW-R

iUniverse, Inc.
Bloomington

How to Hypnotize Your Grandchildren
Easy, Quick, and Fun Ways to Influence the Children in Your Life

iUniverse books may be ordered through booksellers or by contacting:

iUniverse
1663 Liberty Drive
Bloomington, IN 47403
www.iuniverse.com
1-800-Authors (1-800-288-4677)

Because of the dynamic nature of the Internet, any Web addresses or links contained in this book may have changed since publication and may no longer be valid. The views expressed in this work are solely those of the author and do not necessarily reflect the views of the publisher, and the publisher hereby disclaims any responsibility for them.

Any people depicted in stock imagery provided by Thinkstock are models, and such images are being used for illustrative purposes only.

Certain stock imagery © Thinkstock.

ISBN: 978-1-4759-8268-8 (sc)
ISBN: 978-1-4759-8269-5 (e)

Printed in the United States of America

iUniverse rev. date: 4/8/2013

For my grandchildren:
Cash
Dylan
Juniper
Riley
Savannah
Wednesday
Xia

Contents

Acknowledgments

I want to thank my children and their families for their help and support of this book.

Emily Underwood
Megan and Jamie Christian
Sarah and Christopher Fahrbach
Tracy and Patrick Gillespie

Special thanks to my daughter, Tracy Gillespie, for creating the original woodblock artwork shown on the book cover and at the beginning of each chapter. All of the woodblock designs are available as jewelry. Contact Tracy at kitchentableprinter@gmail.com for more information.

Special thanks to my wife, Diana Marie, who provided support and consultation throughout the writing of this book—especially as a grandmother and psychotherapist in the methods of Hawaiian healing arts. She also provided me with information on mandalas, as a certified Mandala Assessment Research Instrument (MARI) practitioner.

Introduction

Complex, dynamic, and often difficult to understand, the relationships adults have with children begin with life itself—first in a mother's womb and forever after the birth of the child. These relationships often begin with the nuclear adult family—the mother, father, siblings, grandparents, and significant others. Then they expand quickly to other individuals, groups, and communities.

Emerging relationships are fun and unique for each child and adult, featuring an infinite number of variables and possibilities, such as familiarity with each other, commonality of interests, and levels of awareness and knowledge. Relationships can be characterized by the following components:

- verbal
- tactile
- olfactory
- auditory
- visual
- imaginary

Nascent relationships, especially for infants, are key factors in a person's lifetime behavior and personality. We adults—mothers, fathers, grandparents, aunts, uncles, teachers, therapists, counselors, and medical professionals—can increase our positive influence on our children before birth, at birth, throughout childhood, and into adulthood.

As a seasoned and licensed social worker, psychotherapist, and hypnotist, I became acutely aware of my influence on the children in my life when I became a grandparent. This feeling emerged after many years of professional experience in the behavioral health field. Additionally, I've taught many college and adult-education courses, published articles, and conducted conference workshops, all of which have enhanced my experience in this field. In 2000, I developed and cofounded a private practice, Alternative Counseling, in my home studio office, to further enhance these growing and divergent treatment options. It is no wonder that, as my grandchildren came along, I found myself in a unique state of astonishment.

My seven grandchildren were born during the last eleven years, and it was then that I began to see, experience, and feel these significant relationships take root and grow. I realized this powerful energy around me provided an opportunity to influence my grandchildren's lives in a positive and significant way. I not only felt that this energy touched my grandchildren but also that it could be expanded to touch everyone—all children and adults— no matter the relationship or environment. Ultimately, this is a book about these critically important early relationships and their effects in one's lifetime.

Increasing our positive influence on our family's future became very important to me. Somehow, and surprisingly, the idea and focus for *How to Hypnotize Your Grandchildren* became evident to me in February 2011, while visiting George Washington's headquarters in nearby Newburgh, New York. There, in the sight and awe of Washington's original desk, I learned from the park guide that George Washington and his staff had a vision for future generations that is clearly documented in history. The guide explained that when Washington knew the Revolutionary War was over, the question loomed: What was to happen next?

As I stood next to his historic desk, I learned that, on June 8, 1783, George Washington wrote a circular letter of farewell to the army, indicating that what was decided at his headquarters would have a far-reaching effect on future generations hundreds of years from that point. We, here and now, are the future generation he was referencing; we are experiencing the effects of his decisions about the formation of our country, the United States of America.

Miraculously, this struck a chord with me about my hopes for the future of my grandchildren and subsequent generations. Perhaps it was how our guide emphasized Washington's concern for future generations and the influences on their beliefs and values; or maybe it was Washington's enthusiasm and the strength of his convictions. Perhaps it was the timing—I had been thinking about the future—or the awakening of my own sense of time and need to move forward in my life.

Whichever the case, the visit sparked a subconscious plan for this book. I felt a connection to George Washington—often thought of as the "father of our country"—and a need to expand my ideas about influencing future generations in a positive way. We are Washington's future generation. Our grandchildren are our future generation and the key to other, more distant generations. They will determine what happens next, and *How to Hypnotize Your Grandchildren* will explain what you can do now to influence your children's behavior and future lives.

What can you teach them today that will have an impact on them twenty, forty, or sixty years from now? Can you influence their beliefs, values, spiritual connections, character traits, and relationships with others and other cultures? Can you have an impact on their family lives and community relationships? Will they be independent, happy, and productive? Will they contribute to society? Will they have fun? Is it possible that what you decide with your grandchildren now will have a profound effect on future generations hundreds of years from now? These questions, and many more, will be discussed in the context of my professional behavioral health background and broad family experience.

How we approach the answers to these questions about our grandchildren will be meaningful and hypnotic. It will apply to all children and our relationships with them. I will explore and demonstrate ways to provide strong, unforgettable, and powerful influences on children. This book will give you the ideas and tools you'll need to have profound, positive effects on your children, both now and in the future. Like Washington's communication to the army, what you teach children now will affect upcoming generations many years from now. Think of the magnitude and responsibility you hold now; it may place you in a state of wonder.

A new generation is created when children are born. As they begin to grow, you can capture and feel their vitality. There is a special relationship, an anticipation of sorts, as you follow accounts of their growth through the weeks and months after they are born. Every day, you sense growth of their minds and bodies, and you sense a new vitality building. Every day, and with every contact, you may experience a new and different relationship with them. They constantly get older, more knowledgeable, and more experienced in their relationships with you and the other adults around them.

This concept of passing time may occur to each child in variable increments, from very small to very large. Adults also change and grow daily in mind and body, although it is usually less perceptible than in children because of age and maturity. Interactions with others are unique slices of life. We can learn to savor them and be mindful of our goals for and influences on others in the future.

Horizontal and vertical time will be explored and experienced. By way of definition, horizontal time refers to time as length and time as age. For example, a one-year-old child will be age five in four years. We all get older moment by moment, day by day, and year by year. On the other hand, vertical time deals with the present experience only. It is what you and your grandchild are experiencing in the here and now, in the current moment. It has no past and no future awareness. For example, awareness and intensity of feelings can be measured in the current moment as vertical time. As a grandparent or significant adult, you will feel a special energy, a feeling that has probably not been felt before. You will feel and experience new interactions as you read this book and as time goes on.

As you read *How to Hypnotize Your Grandchildren,* you may experience different feelings and growth within yourself as you relate to your grandchild. Savor this and consider it fresh verve. You will discover how to use these new feelings in positive and purposeful ways that can make for unforgettable moments in your grandchild's life. One might characterize this as a hypnotic bond, a strengthening of positive energy between two people.

This bond may even be stronger for two related people, but it does not have to be. The strength of the relationship or the bond may depend on the awareness of the individuals involved. You will learn how this energy can be molded, increased, decreased, and nurtured in an infinite number of ways. These creative drives are unique to your relationships. Once you have identified these feelings and energy areas, you will be ready to begin hypnosis and sustain mesmerizing relationships with all the children in your life.

In *How to Hypnotize Your Grandchildren,* you will find that you can nurture your initial feelings into a special hypnotic relationship. Focus on strengthening these relationships through specific mindful and interactive activities, and you will create a calm, loving, creative, and positive environment in which to nurture permanent, positive life skills. Conscious and subconscious behaviors will be explored through fun-filled, meaningful methods.

- You will be introduced to the basic elements of hypnotism and visual imagery.
- You will explore the roles and boundaries of grandparents, children, and grandchildren.
- You will be able to incorporate elements of *lokahi*—the Hawaiian term for aligning the mind, body, and spirit—throughout this experience.
- Through the beginning use of the mandala drawings and introduction of the Mandala Assessment Research Instrument (MARI), you will learn how to nurture children's intuitions and states of consciousness.
- You will learn about approaching soul guidelines with unconditional acceptance, helping to achieve healing, wisdom, and peace.
- You will develop a more mindful attitude in your interactions with others, being further aware of body, mind, and spirit.

In *How to Hypnotize Your Grandchildren*, readers will be introduced to several quick, easy, thoughtful, and interactive hypnotic experiences that can be modified and individualized to take advantage of the infinitely unique circumstances between child and adult. Readers will explore their own creativity and relationships with others, including children, grandchildren, and adults. Individuals have no age requirements or restrictions. Within each activity experience, emphasis will be placed on introducing compelling interventions best suited to the situations at hand. These activity experiences include the following:

- hypnosis
- intuition related to linear and vertical time
- music, vibrations, and dance
- magic and make-believe
- kites and aeronautics
- Superman and other heroes
- visual imagery
- hands-on creative activities

After reading this book, you too will be able to realize its connection to the concepts set forth by General George Washington. His concern for future generations led to a greater vision: that what you do now with your grandchildren will profoundly affect their characters and life circumstances. General Washington was a visionary thinker who was interested in the future. In our time, similar questions about children and the future prevail. This book explores the notion that what you do today with your grandchildren will have deep effects on their behavior and goals for the future.

Hypnosis gives you a more in-depth connection. It shows that special, mindful activities are important tools for relating to children, helping you intensify your interactions with them and their environments. Along with enhancing subconscious activities, your interactions and relationships will grow in current and impending importance and influence. You will learn to use the powers of the adult, the grandparent, and the parent as you amplify hypnotic subconscious thoughts for a greater good.

CHAPTER ONE

What Is Hypnosis and How Does It Work with Children?

The first question is usually: What is hypnosis? Hypnosis may be defined as being in an altered state of awareness, being in a trance, or being in a state of high Suggestibility (Mottin, 2005, 1). Although I concur with and use this definition, definitions of hypnosis are varied and often difficult to understand because of the many misconceptions about hypnosis. Usually, the untrained and general public has these incorrect understandings, creating a mythology around hypnosis. For example, many inexperienced people believe that in hypnosis, your behavior can be controlled, and that you can be made to act like a duck and quack like a duck. This is absolutely not possible and a common falsehood.

The following points about the true nature of hypnosis may clear up some of these disparities and deceptions:

- In hypnosis, a person is always in control and awake. He or she can never be made to do something against his or her will.
- A person must desire to participate in making changes or improving his or her behavior. He or she cannot be tricked into acting in a way that he or she does not want to.
- A common misunderstanding is that a person under hypnosis always tells the truth. Hypnosis is not effective as a lie detector.
- A person will always come out of the hypnotic state. He or she will never be stuck in a hypnotic state.

It's extremely important to clear up these basic myths. The fear of the unknown affects the relationship and can impact the effectiveness of a therapeutic setting. The following is an example from my private hypnosis practice. This story will illustrate that a strong untrue belief about hypnosis can be so powerful that it is often enough to change a person's unwanted behavior even before the actual hypnosis session!

John was a fourteen-year-old boy who was referred to me for fear of entering a vehicle. He had stopped attending school because he was unable to travel by car or bus. He was in the eighth grade and was referred to me by his pediatrician, who lived within walking distance of his home. My office was also within walking distance.

The root of his problem stemmed from a severe car accident at age five and then another recent car accident. He had not attended school for two weeks prior to the visit and therefore was referred to my office. Ironically, he was "cured" of his fear even before seeing me because he believed all of the commonly held myths about hypnosis; he was afraid that I would control his behavior. He did not want to be made to walk like a duck and talk like a duck, so he decided to travel to classes rather than see me.

His only way around seeing me was to start traveling by car or bus and attend school before his first appointment. You might say that he feared me more than traveling by vehicle.

I believe that most young children are already in a state of hypnosis before they see an adult anyway. They live in a fantasy world and are highly suggestible. They are usually ready for fun and games of any form, especially if they're lead by an adult. They believe. They trust. They usually do whatever they're told. They often need boundaries, which adults can easily provide.

Be flexible and be ready to act at a moment's notice. Tune in to their time zone. Tune in to their world, and you can do wonders. For grandchildren and most young children, hypnosis is already working.

What are the basic elements of hypnotism with your grandchildren? This is easy to answer; most young children are already in a hypnotic state simply because they are young children in a fantasy state of mind. They often phase in and out of conscious and subconscious states automatically, at any minute (Mottin, 2005, 13). For example, my four-year-old grandson often makes believe that he is Batman or Superman when he dons his hero shirt or even at the slightest suggestion of any superhero. We can intensify this hypnotism by joining him with our own superhero garb, usually a T-shirt or cap.

Actually, all people can do this, but children seem to do it more easily. Another example of transitioning from conscious to subconscious behavior is inventing a story or reading a fairy-tale book. Children have such fluid, easily manipulated imaginations that you can quickly guide them into any situation or scene. Just the mere verbal or nonverbal suggestion can do this. For example, just tell a four-year-old to make believe that he or she is a cat, and you may immediately see the child crawling on the floor, making the *meow* sound, and acting as a cat. We believe that as you begin to relate to children, you can strengthen your connection with them. This is the secret! Strong and direct communication, both verbal and nonverbal, are the key factors.

As a species, we communicate through verbal and nonverbal interactions, which are both integral to all relationships. Therefore, examine and strengthen these communicative interactions so that they become more efficient, effective, understandable, positive, and fun. We must take a deliberate approach in all our relationships with others, being always aware of body, mind, and spirit within our environment.

As we focus on enhancing our communication connection and awareness of body, mind, and spirit with our grandchildren, we can consider including elements of *lokahi*, the Hawaiian concept for aligning the mind, body, and spirit (Jim, 2005, 12). This may include the language of vibrations and feelings relating to the Hawaiian culture and healing. This concept, or Hawaiian truth, speaks to our sameness and is often difficult to put into words. It may be described as an authentic component of Hawaiian culture. It is not found in writing and is passed on to future generations in nonverbal ways. It addresses basic respect for others, no matter what age (Jim, 2005, 27).

In Hawaiian, emphasis is given to a word by repeating it. *Lomilomi*, which means "energy shift" and "thumb," is an ancient healing art that inspires an energy shift within a person while raising the vibrations of everything and everyone surrounding him or her. It focuses on discovering unity, harmony, happiness, and gratitude with the real self, the spirit, and all mankind (Jim, 2005, 6).

The true meaning of *aloha* is "may the breath of God be in your presence." Just saying the word "aloha" invokes a higher vibration frequency within the body, the temple of lomilomi (Jim, 2005, 25). Aloha imparts a mindfulness of respect, reverence, awareness, truthfulness, clarity, dignity, and warmth in your relationship with others. Through the generations, Hawaiian traditions have been passed on orally and in practice. The awareness of the sacred flow of Hawaiian words carries healing, mystery, beauty, and spiritual depth (Jim, 2005, 26).

You can teach and influence your grandchild about lokahi. Once young children tune their vibrations within themselves, their lives become more balanced and harmonious. Help them feel this wisdom and healing of Hawaii, and they will find purpose and energy in their life.

For example, my six-year-old grandchild was very excited when I introduced her to drumming in our yard. I happened to live along a wooded area and ravine overlooking a small stream. The setting was perfect for the enchanting beat and rhythm of the drum echoing through the trees. We seemed to be hypnotized together as we continued beating our drums in alternating rhythms. Suddenly and without any prompting, she began chanting a beautiful melody unknown to me. My connection to and vibration with her was mesmerizing and sounded like the following:

Hi yo, hi yomae see nee yah.
Hi yo, hi yomae see nee yah.
Hi yo, hi yomae see nee yah.
Hi yo, hi yomae see nee yah.

I asked her about the chant and where it might have originated. She strangely described an Indian tribe and song. I seized this opportunity to talk with her about the elements of lokahi, but it was difficult to do and understand. I was reminded that this teaching is not a special activity or step-by-step process. You do not verbalize and tell it. You show and do it. I don't think that she will ever forget this shared hypnotic moment in time and the wisdom and feeling of aloha between us.

Another example of experiencing the opportunity of lokahi occurred with our grandchild from Vermont. It also involved a drumming activity in her backyard, which was a large field. A campfire helped set the relaxing scene on a beautiful, warm evening. We both had drums and began to rhythmically exchange beats.

I initiated three beats, and she mimicked the same three beats. I drummed for four beats, then one space, and two beats, and she mimicked the same. We continued this way for a bit, and then we switched leads and I mimicked her beats. No words were ever exchanged. We didn't need them.

Again, in this example, I tried to talk about the elements of lokahi, but it was difficult to do and understand. We went with the feeling of the moment in vertical time. We just acknowledged the feelings, smiled, laughed, and enjoyed ourselves. As Kahuna Jim wrote, "We are living in the *paha*, the now" (Jim, 2005, 15).

These experiences seem to permeate everyone involved. We all strive for this feeling of equality; everyone has an equal place, not above or below anyone else. This allows for healing.

One of the most important aspects to think about regarding the health and positive change we hope for our grandchildren is the ability to access intuition. Most of us have never consciously thought about the concept of intuition, its definition, and the use of intuition in the future. At what age does one develop a knowledge or sense of intuition?

Hypnosis, visual imagery, and meditation can be very useful in the development and pursuit of this concept. When developed, we strengthen our sense of self and our relationships to others and to our environment.

It is therefore important to enhance communication and create a hypnotic connection to grandchildren. This can be accomplished through the use of mandala drawings, mentioned earlier. Being aware of the mandala circle drawing concepts will help in nurturing your grandchildren's intuitions and higher self-awareness and states of consciousness. Learning how to access intuition is a learned ability. A more in-depth and accurate view of intuition may be obtained by using a Mandala Assessment Research Instrument (MARI) reading, provided by a certified masters-level social-work professional. In this way, the mandala can be analyzed in terms of color, composition, and other features.

Intuition is a mysterious, powerful, and subtle ability that most people can develop. We are born with an innate capacity for intuition that exists within us. We can learn to ignore it or follow it, to neglect it or nourish it. Intuition holds a high place in relation to our physical and spiritual well-being, our creative self-expression, and our ability to understand ourselves, others, and the experience of life itself. Intuition is not a function of our conscious mind; it is subconscious, quick, and without reasoning or cognizant attention. Similar to instinct and reasoning, intuition is a function that springs from a source deeper than the linear, rational mind. With our intuition, we can perceive the truth and recognize the real nature of a person, a situation, or our own selves. This perception and understanding is something that comes from within us.

One way a child can get in touch with his or her intuition is to create a personal *mandala.* The word mandala means circle or circumference. The idea of using circles and designs within a circle, often with color, is not new in understanding personality.

The Swiss psychiatrist Carl Gustov Jung used the circle as a tool in analyzing his patients. Circle contents often symbolize concentration, personality, and reality (Fincher, 1991, 24). When one creates a mandala, one can experience oneself through a visual portrait of the round and its contents. With a mandala interpretation, children and adults can perceive the truth within and gain better self-understanding. This is what it feels like to experience our intuition.

For example, toward the end of her trip to our home in New York, our grandchild was asked to create a mandala. She was given a sheet of drawing paper, an ordinary pencil, and some colored pencils and crayons, and she was instructed to draw anything she wanted within the circle on the sheet. Figure 1 shows her mandala titled "My Trip to New York." You can draw conclusions about what was important to her about the trip:

- Jones Farm
- butterfly
- pet cat
- lightning bugs in the yard circle
- auntie Sarah
- cousin Savannah
- auntie Emily
- grandpa
- grandmommy
- brother Dylan
- mom
- me

What conclusions can you draw from her personal mandala? Do you get a feeling about her trip to New York? What was important to her? Explain.

Figure 1

From this six-year-olds' mandala, you can see and feel the importance of family, pets, and nature. She included herself, but she placed Jones Farm first and herself last. Nature and animals are important. No one was left out. She has a strong, positive self-concept. Even at age six, she is grounded in her own life and her relationships with others. Her intuition is well established as positive and accurate.

We tried using the mandala drawing with several grandchildren. It was fun, quick, and easy.

For consistency, we developed specific worksheet instructions based on our experience.

Mandala Drawing Worksheet Instructions for the Child

1. Fill in the circle on the sheet of paper, using any of the materials provided: regular pencil, multicolored pencils, paint, and crayons.
2. Draw anything that you want within the circle.
3. What do you think about your personal circle?
4. How does the mandala make you feel?
5. What does the mandala make you believe is important?
6. Do you sense your intuition when looking at your work?
7. Place name, date, and title (if any) on the sheet.
8. Show a top direction (if any) on the sheet

Using the mandala drawing worksheet instructions for the child, we asked our grandchildren to create a mandala. From the drawings, materials used, color selected, and based on responses to the worksheet questions, you may get a sense of their beliefs, ethics, and values. Be mindful that these drawings and responses can be personal and are confidential. They may be written or verbal. The purpose of presenting these drawings here is to give you examples of what you can obtain by using this technique. Individuals of any age may create a mandala. Color is not shown in the examples.

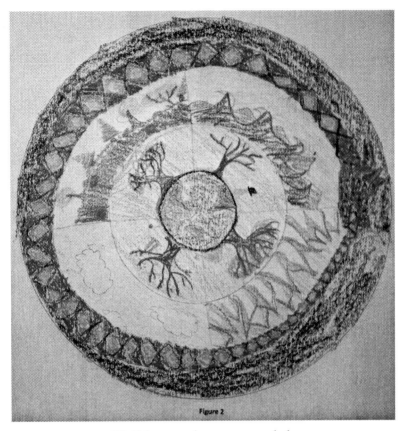

Child, age eleven, mandala

- What do you think about your personal mandala?

- How does the mandala make you feel?

- What does the mandala make you believe is important?

- Do you sense your intuition when looking at your work?

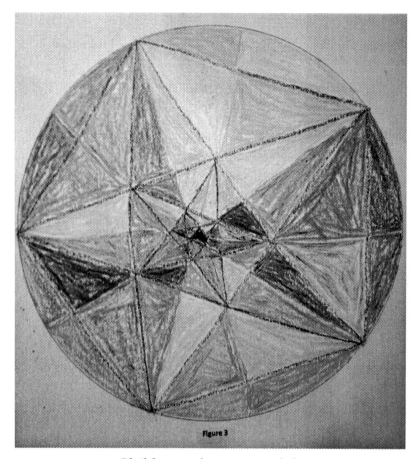

Figure 3

Child, age eleven, mandala

- What do you think about your personal mandala?

- How does the mandala make you feel?

- What does the mandala make you believe is important?

- Do you sense intuition when looking at your work?

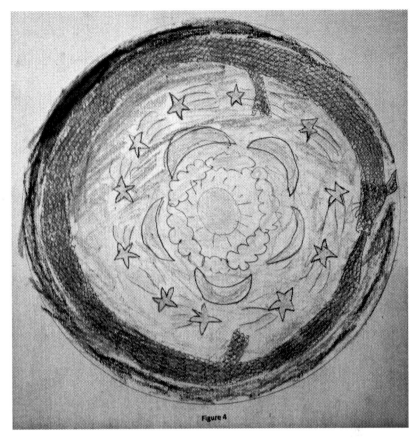

Child, age nine, mandala

- What do you think about your personal mandala?

- How does the mandala make you feel?

- What does the mandala make you believe is important?

- Do you sense your intuition when looking at your work?

Figure 5

Child, age five, mandala

- What do you think about your personal mandala?

- How does the mandala make you feel?

- What does the mandala make you believe is important?

- Do you sense intuition when looking at your work?

Figure 6

Child, age three, mandala

- What do you think about your personal mandala?

- How does the mandala make you feel?

- What does the mandala make you believe is important?

- Do you sense your intuition when looking at your work?

Child, age nine months, mandala

- What do you think about your personal mandala?

- How does the mandala make you feel?

- What does the mandala make you believe is important?

- Do you sense intuition when looking at your work?

It is noted that with children age three and younger, it was probably not possible to obtain a true reading of this drawing exercise. Figure 6 shows the interesting random circular lines created by our three-year-old grandchild. She seemed to just enjoy the moving of pencils and crayons arbitrarily over the paper. For our nine-month-old grandchild, I experimented by designating a volunteer substitute for the baby to do the drawing. I selected a family member, who was familiar with the child's nature, to imagine he or she was the child, and draw a mandala in his place! Figure 7 shows the amazing result. Can you identify characteristics about the nine-month-old child from the artwork? Does the drawing show any characteristics about the family member or the child? If so, how can you tell these characteristics apart?

How old can a child be before hypnotism is useful? Although every situation is different, our grandchild was actually hypnotized at three weeks of age! For example, the child's mother felt he was driving her crazy by wanting to be held constantly. Every time he was placed on the blanket and carpet just outside the room, and not being held, he would cry. The mother felt held hostage by the strong and unyielding tether of her infant. She could not tend to any other tasks because she was always holding her baby.

He was hypnotized by the following actions and words:
- His grandmother slowly and gently picked him up.
- His grandmother simultaneously softly hummed and began singing, "Everyone is right here; everyone is right here; everyone is right here with you." She also gave him a pacifier.
- He immediately stopped crying.
- Comforted by touch, rhythmic and assuring sound, sight (light and shadows), movement, and the feeling of the pacifier in his mouth, he was hypnotized into relaxation—no need to understand words or language.

He was then placed comfortably on the blanket and carpet.

Again, be able to grasp the moment and tune in to the child's rhythm and space. With actions such as these, children can be hypnotized at any age.

CHAPTER TWO

How to Get Started

How do you start hypnotizing your children? Children are already hypnotized just because they are children. You can enhance these entranced states by tuning in to their feelings and circumstances. Most likely, you have already started by simply interacting with them. Every contact and every day will be different. It is useful to be attuned to your children. What do they want to do? What is on their minds? Can you help them meet their agendas? Help them set clear goals about what they want to achieve and let them know what you hope they will achieve. It may be fun for the next minute, hour, or day. What change do you want to make? What are the moods and demeanors of the children and adults?

Answers to these questions will give you direction and purpose. Many tools exist to help you strengthen your bonds with your grandchildren. The roots of these bonds are formed in their spellbound states. You will learn to use these natural energies to maintain and enhance these hypnotized states of being for a long time to come.

Start hypnotizing your grandchild immediately upon your first encounter. Usually, your initial greeting or contact with a person is either by sight (visual) or by sound (auditory). However, it is important not to rule out other senses, such as smell (olfactory) and touch (kinesthetic). It may be all or any combination of these senses. First contacts are important and often set the tone, mood, and intensity of the interactions to come. Be mindful of the following circumstances on your initial contact with your grandchild:

- purpose of the visit
- time of day
- position in the routine schedule (if any)
- location of the visit (the child's own home, another home, a hotel, your home, indoors, outdoors, etc.)
- comfort level of the child
- level of supervision needed and by whom
- expectations of everyone involved, including the child
- approximate length of visit

Since most children are already in a state of hypnosis, the state of your grandchild may be further intensified in the following ways:

- Children learn by repetition. This is often experienced in preschool or school. Children love repetition and feel confident while doing repetitive activities or speaking repetitive phrases. Children want to know that they are growing and making accomplishments. For example, my two-year-old grandchild loves to hear and repeat the exciting expression, "I did it!" or "You did it!" This simple phrase, often repeated in an exciting, loud, drawn-out way, reaffirms her self-worth, growth, and acceptance.

- Consider feelings and emotions. These expressions are very important, and often they create an imprint (Mottin, 2005, 4). An imprint is a thought registered in one's subconscious mind, usually at a time of stress, causing a change in behavior (Mottin, 2005, 4). We all have imprints from the past that affect the way we respond. Imprints are very effectively established in our minds when a statement is made by an authority figure. A grandparent or important adult is extremely influential. A grandparent who understands the power of imprints can use them positively on their grandchildren. By way of an example, here is a positive imprint from my past. My parents told me, "If you stop wetting your bed, we will get you that train set you like in the store window." I stopped wetting the bed, and my parents immediately purchased the train set for me. An imprint may be formed by verbally recognizing and rewarding a positive deed, such as saying, "You did a fantastic job on the drums today! I especially liked the way you made a beautiful beat and rhythm. You were able to communicate your excited feelings to others. Keep up the great work."

- Go with the flow. In many ways, children can communicate their desires nonverbally. For example, when a child wants to be held, the child will melt into your arms and body as if you were one with the child.

Every bend and crack in your body will seem to be filled with the child. If the child suddenly does not want to be held, every crack and bend suddenly opens. It is as if the child disengages automatically, like it or not, and you become unable to hold the sliding and wiggling child down as he or she sinks to the floor. The nonverbal message from your child is crystal clear. "Let go of me and let go of me now!" The child's relaxed and rigid states come and go as needed.

- Focus on the flow. Children have strong attention spans that can lock on an item of interest. Have you ever tried to talk with a child watching Elmo on the television? You will most likely be ignored, or receive a terse no answer. Actually, be aware of how you, as an adult, respond when someone tries to interrupt you! Children are great at mimicking your own ways of responding, or doing what works for them. Be aware of the child's ability to be intensely interested in what is going on. You may not be able to break this attention span.

- Perception is reality. If you believe it, it is true. The belief concepts of children can be magical and are easily implanted in games and relationships. Children step in and out of roles at a mere suggestion. Additionally, children are almost always ready to play. Have you ever heard a child refuse to play a fun game?

- Use positive thoughts. Speak positively, for many thoughts go into the subconscious mind and are accepted literally. For example, suppose the grandparent states, "This room is a pigpen; clean it up." The same situation—a messy room—will probably happen again because the adult claimed and affirmed that the room is a pigpen. This stays in the subconscious mind. Instead, the grandparent might say, "This room has the potential of being neat and orderly. Clean it up." The thought of being clean and orderly stays in the subconscious mind. It is useful to rephrase what we say into a positive communication.

- Be aware of direct and indirect suggestions. For example, the command "Turn off the television" is authoritarian in tone, or mode. The indirect suggestion, or the permission mode, may be "Let's turn off the TV." Another example of a direct suggestion is "May I borrow your pen?" You could rephrase this into an indirect suggestion, such as "Do you have an extra pen?"

As you relate to your grandchildren, it may be useful to create positive anchors for them. An anchor is a cue developed to create a response. It can happen consciously or subconsciously, and it can be positive or negative. It can be something we see, hear, touch, smell, taste, or feel. One way to plant an anchor may be to state to a child, "Every time you see the color red, you will thank your mother for taking you to the party." Other anchors might be "Every time you hear a bird sing, you will drink all of your milk," or "Every time I feel tired, I will clap my hands and feel wide awake." An anchor brings up a memory of an imprint. Don Mottin describes a technique that has helped children reach their goals. He shows how a grandparent can turn sleep into hypnosis. He simply waits until the child falls asleep in his arms, on the couch, or anywhere. As the child is comfortable and falling asleep, but before he or she is actually sleeping, Mottin implants positive suggestions to help the child reach his or her goals (Mottin, 2005, 40–41). The positive suggestion may be about doing better in school, no longer wetting the bed, or any positive concern. The adult may check if the child is getting the message by asking the child to raise his or her finger while the message is given. Practice makes perfect. Many hypnotists use the anchoring technique all the time.

CHAPTER THREE

Positive Interactive Factors

As a grandparent or significant adult, your impact on the children in your life is significant. You are a role model. Everything that you do in their presence—good or bad—is observed and recorded in their memory banks. Be aware of your role at all times. Respect your boundaries as a grandparent, as it is easy to blend and confuse this role with that of the child's parents or significant caregiver. Confusing adult roles will confuse the child's behavior. It is extremely easy to mix up these roles because of differing perceptions, communication styles, beliefs, values, cultural viewpoints, and gender styles. Remember, grandparents are not parents and parents are not grandparents. Do you know the difference?

The differences may be found in the following areas:

- responsibility levels
- final decisions
- rules of life
- cultural values
- boundary definitions

We often want to influence or teach our children right and wrong in all areas of behavior. They are rapidly growing and learning about appropriate behaviors and how lives are lived. What is appropriate in one family may not be appropriate in another. In very young children, learning and growing is a full-time job. As we interact with our grandchildren, we must bring all our energy, knowledge, and influence into the space between the children and us.

The following are two methods of interaction that can be used to help change or influence behavior. Remember, in these circumstances, your goal is to change or modify behavior in the child.

First, let's address the common issue of a child not wanting to go to bed. Children want to have fun and learn, and if left alone, they would probably do this until they dropped from exhaustion. Most very young children do not want to go to bed. A two-year-old does not understand the need for sleep and does not have any ability to implement a schedule. Bedtime usually creates a struggle of wills between adults and children.

We have established that children are already hypnotized, so it is easy to take this concept one step further. This extra step will be fun and quick. Wow! But how?

The key is to move with or create the child's rhythm. The child will begin to slow down when you slow down. Your behavior and attitude are constantly being observed and reflected back to you by the child. Be directive, absolute, and firm in your attitude and actions. Consider the following communication interactions between you and the child:

- Start to slow yourself down at the end of the day, about thirty minutes prior to bedtime, by sitting, lying down, or being quiet. Do not play loud music or make noise or initiate any new activities.
- Yawn or pretend that you are tired and plan to sleep.
- Find time to read a story, tell a story, or review the activities of the day.
- Develop a ritual. Make a repetitive plan of bedtime behaviors, and demonstrate them daily.
- Talk and act softly, rhythmically, and repetitively.
- Talk reservedly about tomorrow's plans and activities. While some children may fall asleep better, some may get more excited thinking about the next day and have more difficulty falling asleep. Use your judgment and know your child.

Remember, the key is to move with or create the child's rhythm. Once you do this, the rest is easy. The child wants to sleep. The child needs to sleep. Sleep is a natural rhythm of the body, and you can help find it. Parents are always amazed by how easy it is for grandparents to put children to sleep. How many times have you said or sent a text message—"*zzzzzzzzzzzzzzzzzzzzzzzzzzzzzz!*"—to the parents that the child or children are sleeping now? Usually, the parents are shocked by this because they do not understand the hypnotic effects of the interactions listed above.

Here's an anecdote to illustrate the benefits of moving with the child's rhythm. One night my grandchild refused to stay in her bed. She was tired after a long, activity-filled day, but she just did not want to be left alone in her bed upstairs while we were downstairs watching a TV show. We moved with her rhythm by simply allowing her to come downstairs with us and lie on the couch while we continued to watch TV. She remained quiet—eyes wide open for a while—and seemed very content. She had no interest in the TV, but she just wanted the feeling of comfort in our space. We did not need to pay any attention to her, nor did she want attention. She was tired at the end of the day. She soon fell asleep. We scooped her up and brought her to bed. She never knew what had happened. Parents can do this too! Again, the philosophy is to move with the child's rhythm.

Guided imagery is another technique that helps change behavior. It is important to use your imagination with this method because you will use your mind to brainstorm any situation. Fun, quick, and easy, it is a form of make-believe that can achieve any goal. You, as the adult, can be the leader and director in setting up the scene. Use your skills and creativity in developing the action, and use your role as the influential adult to give the activity purpose and meaning.

With children, guided imagery may be considered a game, a story, or an adventure. It can be a time for fun, creativity, and entertainment. It can be a learning experience as well. As the adult, you have the full ability to guide the child anywhere! Be positive. Create a balanced and healthy environment. Use the experience as a chance for conducting a very powerful and creative teaching moment. Use the authority of being a grandparent to connect to your grandchildren. This can be a strong hypnotic moment.

Most children are always ready on the spot to begin guided imagery. Just start with a quiet, comfortable location and tell or read a story or script. Choose a story or script to meet a goal that you had in mind for the child. Most scripts are well suited for goals of concentration, relaxation, and rejuvenation. Scripts may be read or paraphrased. You may also freely create your own story, perhaps adapting it to the activities of the day or any unique circumstance of the child. Set a hypnotic tone. Choose a pleasant location and a good time of day that is compatible with the child. Speak in a positive, enthusiastic, and interesting style. Here's an example of a guided imagery script spoken by an adult to a child:

It is time to tell a story about you living in the enchanted forest. Listen and imagine that you and your best friend are walking in the forest. As you are walking, you come across a crystal-clear stream of water. You are thirsty from walking and decide to drink the water. You learn this is magic water, and by drinking it, you may become an adult immediately and travel to any country of your choice in the world!

You and your friend drink, become adults, and decide what country you wish to visit. What country did you choose? What language do you speak? Can you describe your travels and experience in this country? What are the three most important things that you learned in this country?

When you are ready, you may return to your home. Did you bring back any foreign words? Did you bring home gifts? If yes, tell me what they are? Who are the gifts for?

This is only one of hundreds of stories and examples of visual imagery. There are no right or wrong examples, and you are limited only by your imagination. You will find that the child will quickly catch on to the technique and begin to provide visual imageries for you and others. More examples of visual imageries will be provided in chapter eight.

You will be surprised by their imagination and stories. You are providing the lead and example. You will be allowing space for creativity, growth, and learning. You will be instilling self-worth and confidence through what is essentially a compelling feeling. Various techniques are available to enhance this hypnotic feeling and are listed as follows:

- Use of affirmations—An affirmation is a positive statement that is worded in the present tense. It has power and meaning for the one who uses it. Your grandchild can think or say several positive statements. Examples might be:
  1. "I complete my homework every day."
  2. "I remember and understand what I learn and read."
  3. "I am happy being me."
  4. "Every day I feel better than the day before."
  5. "With each game I play, I improve my performance."

- Be aware of the power of words and phrases such as "pretty," "ugly," "big," "small," "good," "bad," "outstanding," "you did it," "great work," "nice job," "I love you," and "you are creative and smart." How do you feel when you use or hear these words?
- Tell children what you want, not what you don't want. For example, try not to say, "Don't play in the street." Say, "Have fun playing in the yard." The word "don't" is often not heard.
- Again, understand the four learning modes:
  1. visual, or seeing
  2. auditory, or hearing
  3. kinesthetic, or feeling by touch
  4. olfactory, or smelling

Don Mottin provides an example of using the visual mode to help a child end bed-wetting. The script below is spoken by the child's parent.

"I know that you are excited about the idea of never wetting the bed again. Before we actually get you to stop wetting the bed, I want to make sure this will make you happy. Close your eyes and you will get to see a very special movie. This movie is special because you will be in it. The movie is starting now. You can see yourself in the movie. You are getting ready for bed. As you see the movie, nod your head 'yes.' Good. Now it is a movie of you sleeping. As you see the movie of yourself sleeping, nod your head 'yes.' You are doing super. Now the movie is about you waking up in the morning. There you are waking up in the morning. You're stretching your arms. Now you're rubbing your eyes. You now notice your bed is dry. Yes, your bed is dry! You jump up and down because you are so happy! You say out loud, 'My bed is dry!' You say it again out loud, 'My bed is dry!' Everyone is so proud of you. How do you like the end of this movie?" (Mottin, 2005, 51–52)

- Use the power of suggestion. A common example of the power of suggestion is the Light and Heavy Arm Test. In this exercise, ask the child to stand with both arms extended out, parallel to the floor or ground. While his or her eyes are closed, tap the right wrist slightly, indicating that you are tying a string around the wrist and attaching a helium balloon that floats up into the air. Do the same for the left wrist, except with this one, indicate that you are attaching a very heavy bucket filled with wet sand. Talk about the right arm getting lighter and lighter and being lifted up by the helium balloon. Talk about the left arm moving down, weighted by the heavy, sand-filled bucket. As the right arm goes higher and higher, the left arm goes lower and lower. After only a few minutes, ask the child to stop, and tell him or her, "Without moving your arms, open your eyes and see where your arms are. Your right arm will be raised up high and feel light. Your left arm will be down and feel heavy."

In this exercise, the power of suggestion uses touch on each wrist. Every child and adult is different, just as every response may be different. Follow the child's lead and deliver the suggestions based on how the child is responding. The key words are "light" and "heavy." It is important to have fun and reward the child for how well he or she has done. Give the child praise for doing a good job. A successful exercise will strengthen future hypnotic successes.

The power of suggestion is very important and can be used in many circumstances to change unwanted behaviors. A simple script, which can easily be expanded, involves rewiring the brain so that the desired behavior is achieved. For example, if you want to help your grandchild not to fear a visit to the doctor, consider this hypnotic script:

> "Now, we know that you have had a fear of going to the doctor in the past, and you want to stop having that fear. Is that correct?"
>
> *Child nods his or her head yes.*
>
> "Because your brain determines all your fears and activities, I want you to take this rewiring tool and rewire your brain in such a way that you no longer have this fear."

Child takes the imaginary tool and places it against his or her head, pretending to fix the wiring. (The child actually perceives that he or she is adjusting the brain wires.) Child signals when the rewiring job is finished. Child no longer has this fear.

It is interesting for me to describe an incident when this power of suggestion was used—by my three-year-old grandchild!—to help me with an injury. I accidentally bumped my head on a low wood beam while playing with her at Jones Farm. Although it hurt, I was not injured. Later in the day, she was playing doctor with her toy stethoscope, placing the toy on her heart and stomach, so I asked her to check my heart with the toy instrument. She would not check my heart. She remembered that I had bumped my head earlier in the day and immediately placed the stethoscope on my injury. I was healed! I felt much better emotionally and physically. I was hypnotized by my grandchild!

CHAPTER FOUR

Intuition and Linear and Vertical Time

Most of us are aware of linear time. From the time we are born to the time we die, a calendar marks the seconds, minutes, hours, days, and years as a measurement of longevity. From infancy to old age, we live in one direction—from young to old. The average age a human lives to is seventy-eight years old.

Linear time moves second by second; it is not still. It constantly moves on, always changing and aging us. It builds upon itself and creates a history and a sense of the past. Linear time is never the same. It creates a different and unique space in time. We have no influence on its speed.

Vertical time is here and now. It is time in the current moment. There is no past. There is no future. It is now, in the present. When we consider the focus of vertical time with our grandchildren, we can see and open in-depth possibilities. Imagine the concept of freezing the moment and savoring the vertical time with your grandchild. Picture the possibilities of a relationship and a connection full of communication, feeling, energy, and spirit. When you focus on your current feelings and relationship, you intensify your here-and-now thoughts and feelings with the child. You become well connected and cognizant of your emotional state. You have increased your association and mindfulness level. Communication is heightened. Feelings are amplified. Energy levels are increased. Spirit may emerge as an additional association link with the child. All or some of these relationship opportunities are possible.

Experiencing vertical time with children is extremely important; all focus is on the here and now. There is no concept of former or upcoming or the accompanying issues. You are existing in the moment. Most young children have very little problem doing this and do it all the time anyway.

As an adult, you have the ability to strengthen the moment. Stop and think about how you can increase the quality of your interaction and relationship. You may have to train yourself to do this with the following methods:

- Brainstorm the goals of your interaction.
- Think of the probable end result of your interaction.
- Place yourself in the child's shoes.
- Focus on feelings.
- Listen to the child and what he or she wants to do.
- Place value on what he or she says.

If you mention any activity or game to a child, he or she will usually want to do it right now. He or she will disregard all rationales or reasons for delaying the activity. This is because children are immediately ready to live in vertical time; this seems to be the most important time to a young child. It is often more difficult for an adult to move into this time with the child. As an adult, it might be better to plan to initiate an interaction with plenty of time to experience it. Be ready to implement the interaction instantly. Delaying a suggested interaction may lessen your hypnotic sense over time. In other words, the child is ready to begin the activity instantaneously and is already hypnotized. It seems that the only less-than-positive reason for this situation is that it is not realistic. If possible, time your interactions so that you can play the game or activity immediately. In this way, you can seize the moment, as it were, with the child who's already hypnotized and in vertical time.

To illustrate, here's an example of an activity in vertical time: I suggested to my granddaughter that we play hide-and-seek. She quickly said, "Okay," and immediately began playing. We alternated being the hider and the seeker. We were both entranced at that moment and had fun enjoying the imminence of the game. It is interesting to note that the game usually ends as quickly as it begins. Suddenly the child decides to stop the game or shift into another game or activity. If you go along with it, it is your opportunity to relish in more vertical time. With vertical time such as this, you spontaneously move together and key off of each other's creativity and excitement. Have fun and enjoy the captive moment.

I do not think it is possible to write a book about hypnotizing children without including the circus. The circus is a mesmerizing event that appeals to children of all ages. Both linear and vertical time are experienced, since the anticipation of going to the circus and the overall involvement of being at the circus can be so powerful that another time concept is seemingly created. Rich in history, romance, action, and color, the circus has it all, including music, dancing, entertainment acts, showmanship, animals, and magic tricks, often presented simultaneously in three rings. Take your children to the circus and you will automatically be spellbound. Dating back in America to 1884 and developed by the Ringling Brothers and others, the circus has earned the name as The Greatest Show on Earth. (North, 1960, 76). Today, in addition to the circus, be cognizant of the many entertaining and influential shows and forums available to children. Many of these inputs and venues into the child's mind and experience are controversial. Examples of these environmental experiences include television, computer input, movies, and amusements parks, to name a few. Parents often monitor, expose, or restrict such input, mostly in accordance with their adult parenting beliefs and values. Be aware of the differing impact and intensity of horizontal and vertical time as it relates to the child's learning and experience.

CHAPTER FIVE

Magic and Make-Believe

Magic and make-believe mixed with perception and reality can be extremely powerful. Add the components of timing, circumstance, and opportunity, and you will have hypnotic skills at your fingertips. Always be ready to grab the opportunity. One such time came to light during my grandchild's visit to our house during the holidays.

All three grandchildren spent the day with their parents at the Museum of Natural History in New York City. The youngest, age eight, was extremely excited about the trip and seeing the dinosaur and fossils exhibit. She had studied fossils in school and was primed for a great visit with us. The next day, she actually found and identified a fossil in our yard. She was excited about this find, as were the rest of us. She could not wait to bring her fossil to school and show her friends. All she wanted to do was tell her friends about the trip.

Several hours after her great fossil find, she could not find it. Everyone in the family looked everywhere, but the fossil was lost. She was devastated. This was a sad state of affairs. It was time to hypnotize!

The circumstances and timing were right for finding this fossil. We knew it had to be somewhere in the house. It was time to call on all of our energy and hypnotic powers and focus on a creative way to locate the prize. That night we called a special family meeting at eight o'clock, in the living room, to discuss the following plan:

- All members heard a description of the fossil from the eight-year-old, describing the nature of the item and its importance. She also said where she had looked for the fossil.

- We discussed how the mind and body are connected and how mental energy can affect physical energy in our body and nature.

- I demonstrated a magic trick called the Haunted Key. I took a skeleton key off of my key ring and placed it in the palm of my hand. I asked all at the meeting to think, *Turn, key, turn.* This command was silently thought over and over again until the key actually turned in the palm of my hand. The key trick proved and emphasized that the mind and body are truly connected. It also added to the ceremonial nature of the special family meeting.

- It was then time for everyone to silently meditate that the fossil would be found and that someone in the group would know the location of the fossil before or

when they woke up in the morning. I asked everyone
to go to bed thinking about the fossil and its location.

The next morning, our grandchild's mother Tracy woke up at
about seven o'clock, looked under the edge of the rug near her bed
and the piano, and found the fossil. She told everyone that she had
had a feeling about it when she woke up. She just looked, and there
it was! She had found it wedged in a crevice under the bed.

The children were immediately spellbound. They were very
quiet and seemed to be in a state of wonderment. I am sure that,
to this day, this memory and feeling of wonder will be embedded
in their minds. Our eight-year-old, Xia, was especially happy, as
she got her prized possession back. She may still have the fossil to
this day!

Playing with dollhouses filled with pretend people and
furnishings is a very easy way to hypnotize children and keep them
mesmerized. Introduce a dollhouse to your grandchildren, and
their imaginations will be carried away by countless creative stories
and fantasies. Stories can be invented, magic and make-believe
may occur, or real-life adventures may be enacted. Dollhouses
provide a forum for psychodrama where issues and concerns can
be dramatically acted or played out.

I am sure that any dollhouse will work. Today, many types
of dollhouses and furnishings are on the market. My favorite
type of dollhouse is the old-fashioned wooden kit, which can be
constructed with glue. If the children are old enough, they can
help build it. It can then be painted and decorated with wallpaper,
curtains, and flooring. Some houses add battery-powered electric
lighting. I believe the more details, the more enthralling the
dollhouse. I remember a dollhouse that had a lounge chair and
magazine rack in the living room. Looking closer, the magazine
rack contained a family photo album. The photos were actual

photos of the grandchildren (cousins and friends) who had played with the dollhouse.

As a grandparent hypnotist, you have great latitude and power to set the platform for all sorts of interactions. Use your knowledge of the child and his or her interests, beliefs, values, and future plans to help guide his or her growth and wisdom. For example, you may set the stage (the dollhouse) in the following way:

- Provide a family setting to match the child's family's situation, including similar family members, friends, pets, and living environment.
- Choose a relatable location or event time. For example, "Your family is planning a picnic at the park this afternoon," or "Plan and prepare for a birthday party tomorrow."

It is often best to let the children set the stage and determine their own ideas and fantasies. They are now automatically hypnotized with this activity and are often impervious to people around them. Dollhouses are mesmerizing.

CHAPTER SIX

Kites and Aeronautics

Kites are fabulous. In fact, today you can become hypnotized just by buying a kite. The varieties are infinite, and they often incorporate various themes, including pictures and symbols of heroes, famous people, insects, animals, and other topics. While on vacation on Long Beach Island in New Jersey, we stopped at a local department store and found all kinds of amazing kites. We bought a 3-D nylon Top Gun airplane with a fourteen-inch wingspan, twine, and a winder. The kite was especially useful for connecting with our three-and-a-half-year-old grandson. His great-grandfather had been a pilot in the air force. What a great compelling connection and learning experience it was for him to learn how to fly this kite and talk about his great-grandfather. We also got him a Superman kite, which provided another valuable hypnotic connection. It was important to instill a sense of power and self-esteem, connecting the past and future.

We also bought two insect kites, a ladybug and butterfly. These were very colorful and easy to fly. These types of kites are excellent entrancing connections for those grandparents who collected insects when they were young. They are also a great way to teach about insects and their places in nature. *Can you identify the four stages and order of butterfly growth—egg, larva, pupa, and adult? How many legs does a ladybug beetle have? On the kite you can see it has six legs.*

When flying kites, we must be mindful of the many warning labels and informational instructions on the kite package. For example, the Top Gun kite package indicated that "parental guidance is recommended when flown by children eight years old and younger." Also noted on the package was the Kite Flyer's Code for Safe Flying:

Never fly the kite in thunderstorms, rain, or violent winds.

Never fly the kite near electric lines, highways, or airports.

Never fly the kite in a crowded area since the kite crashing down can hurt people.

Parks or beaches are ideal flying sites to fly a kite.

Kite-wind ratings were also listed on the package and proved to be important. Our ladybug beetle was rated for five to fifteen miles per hour (mph). The age group requiring parental guidance for this kite was three years old and older. Our two-and-a-half-year-old grandchild did well with the sub-five-mph wind. We were not able to fly the kite because it was too windy on the beach. It is important to be mindful of the child's age and the wind conditions.

Actually, what really happened on one windy day was that she soon lost interest in the kite. She was more interested in playing in the sand with her pail and shovel. Her father became absorbed by the kite to the point where he took hold of the kite line and picked up on the kite-flying fun. Kite flying provides an opportunity to send messages up into the universe! You can send a message by writing a note on a piece of paper and attaching it securely but loosely to the kite line so that it quickly rises up the line, on its own, to the kite. Figure 8 shows an example of a message and how it is cut so that it can be attached to the kite line. Cut along the line and use your imagination as to what message to send up into the universe. Examples of communications include

- "I love my family";
- any wishes for love, success, and happiness;
- "Help me find a star";
- "Help me with math";
- "I'd like watermelon for dessert."

Enjoy the day. Kite flying is a great experience. To experience kite flying for the first time is a special growth skill. Do not be afraid to give your child the cord handle. He or she will be immediately hypnotized having total control of the kite. What a wonderful first time feeling of power, control, and self-confidence. All who are nearby will be entranced, even the spectators. This is an experience not to be missed.

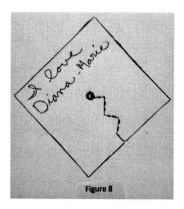

Figure 8

Use the kite-flying experience to teach and talk about other related flying topics. Many opportunities exist for introducing topics such as:

- clouds
- sun
- airplanes
- spaceships and travel
- weather conditions
- gravity
- earth
- birds
- pilots and astronauts
- stars
- an infinite variety of related outer space topics

It is important to show how various topic and interest areas can be expanded, or contracted or related to other themes as needed. Always be on the lookout for teaching opportunities and ways to make a fun and meaningful impact. Look for the spellbinding moments and make them happen. If you do, you will be a grandparent in demand. Grandchildren and all children will be drawn to you like magnets!

CHAPTER SEVEN

Music, Vibrations, and Dance

Sounds are vibrations. Musical vibrations are important aspects of communication and are especially vivid in connecting to young children. Children already have a sense of rhythm and movement. Forming connections through vibrations with children can help to achieve change and positive growth. Communication through vibration brings us closer to the earth's natural rhythms by helping us be mindful of the daily revolutions of the earth and orbits of the planets. This helps us relate closely to how we feel and grow. It can make us aware of how our rhythms mimic nature both around us and inside of us. Further, it relates to the rhythms of our breathing, our heartbeat, our sleep patterns, our exercise routines, our nutritional needs, and our spiritual thoughts. We naturally seek to become one with nature and at peace in spirit.

To enhance these goals in children, adults can use musical instruments, such as drums, flutes, and conch shells. These vibration instruments and the sounds they make have been in existence for many years, dating back to ancient history. Music and tempos are therapeutic and hypnotic. Sounds and vibrations touch our very souls, helping us become more relaxed and centered. Music helps clear our minds and identify our goals. Musical instruments, which balance vibrations, are mesmerizing in every sense and can provide a cathartic mechanism. Finding balance in life and peace of mind can be very powerful tools for young children to attain equilibrium and harmony. Finding this balance will bring forth the energy and inspiration to forge a natural way of life. It is good to be attuned with nature.

A quick, fun, and easy way to connect with children is to have drums, flutes, and other instruments readily available. In this way, you can benefit from tuning in to your grandchild's state of readiness, taking advantage of natural hypnotic moments.

I remember speaking with my eight-year-old grandchild about a very exciting, happy moment at the Tunbridge World's Fair in Tunbridge, Vermont, where she won a ribbon for exhibiting a creative piece of art. She was so excited and happy to talk about it the next day at home; she was already enthralled by the thought of it. I was able to take this happiness one step further by suggesting that she drum her happiness and excitement. I brought out several drums from my car and asked her to express her happiness and excitement by choosing a drum. She began to use it, and before long, her ten-year-old twin sisters and the rest of her family were drumming sounds of happiness and excitement.

In a short time, other feelings were expressed—wonder, amazement, laughter, fear, sadness, peace, boldness, luck, creativity, and much more. The experience led to sound games, including follow-the-leader, the fun and creative game where one person mimics the sound of the other. The whole family became involved, as any surface could be turned into a drum.

How do you drum happiness and excitement? Try it! You will be surprised by the rhythm and sounds! Everyone is different. How does your grandchild sound?

I like playing the conch shell. This is a very large seashell, often found in Hawaii, the South Seas, or the Caribbean. A bugle-sized hole is cut at the end of the shell, creating a channel for airflow, much like a brass musical instrument. I believe it is very hypnotic and therapeutic, especially if one is able to play it. Historically, the use of this shell goes back many centuries. Often it was used to begin ceremonies, announce activities, or begin battles, depending on the time and culture.

Although I love this instrument, I found it difficult to learn. I struggled to create a bugle sound by vibrating and pursing my lips in a way that resonated throughout the shell. When done right, the sound is beautiful. One large vibrating sound can often be echoed throughout your body, shell, and hillside. It took me about a year of practice before I could reach a satisfactory sound. My eight-year-old grandchild was able to play the magnificent note with one try and in less than one minute. She became one with the shell. She was spellbound. Another way to create sounds with the shell is to blow into it to create the sound of the sea and crashing waves. This can provide a soothing and therapeutic feeling of returning to the sea.

Another effective and positive vibration tool is singing. Our bodies are musical instruments; our voices create a unique vibration sound. Singing songs alone or in groups is fun, pleasurable, and hypnotic. Individuals sing, families sing, and large groups sing.

Introduce dance and body movement to your grandchildren, and they are immediately hypnotized. Children like to move. They enjoy moving their bodies—their hands, toes, and all—especially to a beat or rhythm. Children like the attention, uniqueness, and feel of moving. They like to mimic an adult and learn to use their body parts to dance and move. A movement exercise can be impromptu, simple, and done on the spot with any young child. It can be geared to the child's age and interest.

This simple exercise provided an interesting, fun, and quick result for our grandchild:

> "Now, grandchildren, stand in front of me and put your feet apart like this. Put your hands up into the air. You mimic what I do. Hands up, hands down, hands out, left hand up, and all hands down. Sit down; stand up; stand with right foot; clap your hands; freeze!"
> *Stop all movement.*
> "Start your movement again, and turn around."

As you can see, commands are simple, endless, and fun. Be creative—add sound, quack like a duck, sing, dance, or clap. Switch and alternate leadership between yourself and the child.

You can play the game Simon Says by adding this dimension to the activity and omitting the phrase "Simon says" as desired.

Discuss feelings and movement after the activity.

This simple and straightforward type of activity is not only enjoyable but it can also develop a sense of rhythm, body awareness, and socialization. Sound can be added to any of these activities, creating further excitement. Sound can be in the form of music, singing, humming, clapping, and tapping. Be creative. You and your grandchildren will be hypnotized.

Dance, rhythm, movement, and sound combinations can be dated back for centuries. Dance provides

- expressions of grace;
- stress reduction;
- positive feelings;
- relaxation;
- a sense of well-being;
- self-awareness;
- confidence;
- beauty;
- originality.

All of these benefits can be achieved without the spoken word. Dance creates a hypnotic spell, bringing greater harmony of the body, mind, and spirit. It is a great form of expressing happiness, fear, and other feelings. You and your grandchild can create a unique dance activity. Add breathing exercises, visualizations, relaxation, storytelling, poetry, masks, costumes, singing, and exercise. The interactions between child and adult, child and child, and group and child usually inspire increased social and interactive skills as well as self-assurance, pride, and inspiration.

CHAPTER EIGHT

Superman and Other Heroes

Our three-and-a-half-year-old grandchild's favorite hero is Superman. This old-time hero was and still is my favorite too. Superman's motto is "Truth, justice, and the American way." The well-known character is the secret identity of reporter Clark Kent, who, when needed to fight crime or save the world, hides himself in a telephone booth and strips off his suit and tie, revealing the Superman outfit of blue and red. Superman then flies through the air to stop crime and save people with his superhuman strength.

Having seen him in his Superman shirt in several photos, I knew this hero was important to my grandson. When his family planned a trip to visit us in New York, I seized the opportunity to pick the family up at Newark Liberty International Airport.

I bought a Superman shirt and wore it to the airport. I actually felt great as the only costumed superhero at the airport and managed to get several positive comments and stares. My wife, Diana, accompanied me and stated that she felt good being with Superman as his girlfriend, Lois Lane. She actually took on the role of Lois, and it was fun! People at the airport asked me for directions and other types of help!

My grandson caught sight of me in the Superman shirt and seemed shocked that his grandfather might actually be Superman. He was completely and totally hypnotized on the spot. He stuck with me the whole time on our trip home and during the entire week of his visit.

We all need heroes and heroines in our lives. We need them to look up to so that we can aspire to greater things. Heroes are often larger than life; they transcend the self. Heroes often serve as the model of what we want to be; they represent a higher level of life and spirit. They take us out of our everyday lives and lead us to a place of hope and personal power. They motivate us to take charge and go forward with purpose. Heroes inspire us to help others and guide us to believe that we can make a change for the better in this world.

How do you find your hero? One rainy day, during my grandson's visit, we took a trip to our local bookstore. In the children's books section of the store, we found the shelves bursting with superheroes of every variety. We actually looked for and easily found our mutual hero, Superman! What a pleasure it was to look at the pictures of Superman flying through the air to halt crime and save people with his superhuman power. We also saw pictures of him as Clark Kent. We found many other superheroes and what they stand for as well. There are many other superheroes to inspire children.

- **Wonder Woman** has strength and power. She fights to protect those in need.
- **Batman** fights crime in Gotham City and keeps the citizens safe.
- **Green Lantern** keeps peace, order, and justice in the universe. It is the highest honor and responsibility.
- **Captain America** is America's secret weapon committed to defending America's ideals.
- **The Amazing Spider-Man** fights all evil.
- **The Lone Ranger** uses only silver bullets to fight outlaws.

Did you find your hero in the list above? Does it make you think about what kind of hero you want or need in your life? Heroes can be actual living beings, human, animal, spiritual, or historical. Your hero might be a member of your family, a relative, or a person in your workplace, neighborhood, or community. Do you have a hero or heroine whom you know personally? What is it about your hero or heroine that you like? What traits does he or she have that make you feel safe and lead you to a place of inspiration and courage in your own life?

It is worth thinking about. Another way to look at it is that you can be someone's hero or heroine too. Write down the characteristics or values that motivate you. What gives you energy and strength on all levels? Once you are aware of those qualities, you can emulate the superhero that you want to be. Then, wow! The changes in your life will come faster than a speeding bullet. If you want to find the hero or heroine within you, let the power be with you.

Playing Santa Claus has its pleasures and responsibilities. As a former Santa Claus of Gimbels, Woodbury Common Premium Outlets, the United States Military Academy, numerous private parties, and for my own grandchildren, I can tell you that a person dressed as Santa Claus automatically hypnotizes each child and adult he meets. Children are in wonder when they see or hear Santa Claus. Perception is reality, and as Santa Claus, I automatically played the role when my suit was on. It was actually impossible for me not to act and sound like Santa. The role of Santa was so strong that, when I was receiving the children, I could not use my normal voice and demeanor. I was always in character, even when others, always adults, spoke to me as if I weren't in character.

I even felt like Santa Claus, a celebrity commanding attention, admiration, and spiritual awe. What a worthy feeling to be this important figure. I did not want to let the children down; after all, I was Santa Claus, and I acted as Santa Claus. I had a very strong sense of responsibility. I also felt privileged to enter another person's cultural, spiritual, and personal imagination. I was perceived as real by all children, and they all seemed instantly captivated. They listened to what I said, and they all could be molded by the experience of seeing Santa. A snapshot picture confirmed the meeting.

Santa is a great hero, and all who have contact with him are in a mesmerizing state. What a great opportunity Santa presents to build the character of children now and in the future!

CHAPTER NINE

Visual Imagery with Children

Visual imagery with children is, essentially, storytelling. Stories can be easily crafted and adapted to any situation. Your rhythm, pace, inflection, and mannerisms are important when telling stories.

A common time for stories is right before going to sleep. Stories can be invented from that day's activities or the rhythm of nature and the earth. We told our grandson a bedtime story, adapted from a movie he had seen the day before, in an effort to help him go to sleep. The movie, *Zookeeper*, features talking zoo animals that help the zookeeper find true love. It is a beautiful fantasy.

We set his bedtime story in our front yard, where the insects, butterflies, lightning bugs, dragonflies, and forest animals met at a certain time to race across the lawn. At the start of the race, each animal made a certain sound and talked about winning. A fairy stood at the finish line; she ended the race with sleepy ideas and then faded away until everyone was sleeping. Our grandson was hypnotized and sleeping within minutes! We are sure he had very pleasant dreams.

Helping children fall asleep sometimes involves dealing with the bad witch, who keeps children up all night. Good witch, bad witch—which witch is your witch? Our grandchildren often had trouble falling to sleep because the bad witch was holed up in their bedroom. The bad witch made scary noises and sounds, preventing the children from sleeping. This sleepless condition went on for months until we decided it was time to counter the bad witch by introducing a good witch. On our next visit to their home in Vermont, we decided to find and bring along a good witch, purchased in a local New York toy store. We gave the good witch some compelling attributes, such as making sure she was a little bigger and therefore tougher than the bad witch. We even gave the good witch special powers to make the bad witch harmless and ineffective. We made up a bedtime story and talked about how the good witch was in charge now and forever. The children were hypnotized. The children were sleeping! Their parents were happy.

CHAPTER TEN

Hands-on Creative Activity

Using your own intuition and unique nature is one of the most exciting aspects of hypnotizing children. It is this aspect that may give the most satisfaction because you'll be drawing on your own interests, knowledge, and experience and sharing all or parts of yourself by teaching, showing, and explaining who you are. It does not matter what specific interest or activity you focus on. What is important is that you love the activities and transfer that love to your grandchildren. They will know and sense your love, and they'll absorb the activity. In the process, they will most certainly be hypnotized.

Here are just some of the possible spellbinding tools and activities:

- Puppets—Puppets are exciting and dramatic tools for relating to children. Puppets are fun and portable, and they hypnotize children immediately. Most children are eager to play and dramatize stories; they can easily act out their lives and feelings in playacting with puppets. As a hypnotist of children, you may want to collect a large variety of puppets and have them readily available for puppet shows. I like hand puppets and keep several on hand wherever I go. I usually keep them in a gym bag and in my car. Puppets can be thematic and can include representative people in all walks of life, as well as animals, insects, and fictional characters. Plays and stories stem from the use of puppets; the possibilities are endless. Let the show begin!

- Magic tricks—Magic provides an exciting and theatrical way to relate to children. Children are easily hypnotized with an endless variety of tricks and magic shows. Cards, coins, and bubbles are easy to find, and I use all three for my magic act. Remember that practice makes perfect. I keep at least a dozen tricks up my sleeve at all times and for any occasion.

- Games—Games are great for children. They can be simple or complex. They can be played inside or outside. They are quick, easy, and fun. My grandchildren love to play the following games:

hide-and-seek	cards
shadow tag	hopscotch
tag	Monopoly
pin the tail on the donkey	pick-up sticks
ball	marbles
tic-tac-toe	jump rope

- Show-and-tell—Show-and-tell provides a brilliant way for children to satisfy their need to tell adults about what they have learned and experienced. They need adults to listen to them. Just ask a child to show you his or her outfit, game, toy, activity, or new knowledge from school, and you will have an entrancing effect on him or her. One of our grandchildren gives us daily reports of her new songs, dance steps, letters learned, and games played.

- Arts and crafts—Creating and working on a project together with a child is a hypnotizing activity. The possibilities and projects are infinite, ranging from homemade creations to purchased products. Adults can instantly be ready if they have glue, scissors, tape, crayons, pencils, paints, and paper. Add some creative ideas and imagination, and you have an afternoon's worth of activities ready to go!

- Hands-on creative activity is a wide-open grouping and includes whatever you and the child decide to do. Many factors may be involved in the activity decision including skill level, fun level, interests, desires, feelings, degree of difficulty, creativity, and motivation, just to name a few. I believe it is worthy to teach and expand a child's skills and experiences. Since you, as an adult, may have more knowledge and experience, it may be easier for you to use what you know best, enjoy, and have found valuable. For example, I can remember to this day that my cousin George introduced me to stamp collecting. He was ten years older than I was and known as the stamp collector in our family. One day when I was about eight years old and after he showed me his collection, he gave me a starter stamp album and many of his duplicate stamps. I was hypnotized. As a member of the American Philatelic Society today, I continue to collect stamps and thank him for opening my eyes to United States and world history, friends, stamp shows, and countless fun times through stamps.

Take a few minutes to brainstorm some ideas such as these:

- sports—baseball, soccer, volleyball, golf, tennis, sledding, snowshoeing
- gardening—flowers, vegetables, birdhouse gourds, beekeeping, fruit trees, birds
- rock, mineral, and fossil collecting; insect collecting; coin collecting; book reading
- stargazing, seashells, tree identification, knot tying, fishing, fly tying
- travel—land, sea, air, universe exploration (I knew a grandfather who, once a year, asked a different grandchild to select any country in the world to visit. He then proceeded to make travel vacation arrangements to visit that country with his grandchild!)

Know yourself and determine what you can add to this list. You may be surprised that the list may actually include what you wish you can do. Imagine how it would be if you can learn a new idea or activity together with your grandchild. All of this may be added to your grandchild's ideas. The possibilities are exciting and infinite! In fact, what you may find is that your mesmeric relationships with others will become second nature to you—that every interaction will be special and have a heightened meaning and influence. It will become part of you and be who you are.

Conclusion

I believe that teaching young children is a natural and instinctual process that calls upon past experiences and influences the future. As in the days of General George Washington, ideas and decisions made today will affect and influence the lives of future generations. This concept is true for today's grandparents as they teach and interact with children.

Grandparents and significant adults are in a special position to impart and instill beliefs and values. There is a magical connection between adults and children. Therefore, adults must be especially mindful of their important roles and abilities to influence the young. It is important to recognize and use this great, influential, hypnotic power in a positive and careful way. This is a special time. Embrace it, and do not waste it. Realize that this connection is in existence, whether you want it or not, whether you realize it or not, and whether you use it or not. Be positive at all times. You are the role model, observed and analyzed in everything you do.

Every relationship is different; adults and children are different. Relationships can be handcrafted bonds between children and adults; two or more personalities connect, forming constructive experiences of growth, warmth, and excitement for learning. Character-building principles and ethics are taught, transferred, and incorporated into the heart and soul of a child.

I hope you have learned and can better demonstrate some of the countless examples of magical relationships possible with children.

I hope you have gained more ideas about how to communicate better and improve your bond with children. Connecting with another human being can be easy, simple, and fun. Hypnosis and visual imagery have had a significant effect on our connection with our grandchildren. I hope they will magnify and energize your relationship with all children and adults. You can absolutely affect the future lives of children and adults for generations to come.

I am confident that you have learned how to get started and how to meet and share with children on their terms, sensing their rhythms and needs. By doing this, I anticipate your success in entering their world, providing a magnetic interaction that will lead to their personal growth.

I am optimistic that you have learned about the importance of boundaries for grandparents, parents, and grandchildren. Children need boundaries as an extension of love and safety. Boundaries shape behavior and impact on the growth of self-worth.

By using the mandala sketches, I hope you have been familiarized to a way of nurturing children's intuitions and higher states of self and consciousness. You are now aware of emotion guidelines and unconditional acceptance. You are aware of how to achieve healing, wisdom, and peace. By adopting ideas from this book, I am confident that you will be able to explore a more expressive approach in your interactions with others and be more aware of body, mind, and spirit within your grandchildren's environment. I believe that you may reach a state of amplified awareness to those around you. Your heightened sensitivity may become part of your everyday actions, lifestyle, and personality to the point where you will not have to think about it. It will become part of you. It will affect future generations.

Go forward, have fun, learn, grow, and do worthy things.

The author's seven grandchildren, December 2012

References

Campbell, Don G. *The Mozart Effect*. HarperCollins Publishers, Inc., 2001

Carroll, Lee, and Jan Tober. *The Indigo Children*. Carlsbad, CA: Hay House, Inc.,1999.

Cleary, David A. *George Washington's First War*. New York: Simon and Schuster, 2011.

Fast, Julius. *Body Language*. New York: Pocket Books, 1970.

Feinstein, David. *Energy Psychology Interactive Self-Help Guide*. Ashland, OR: Intersource, 2003.

Fincher, Susanne F. *Creating Mandalas*. Boston: Shambala Publications, 1991.

Friedman, Robert Lawrence. *The Healing Power of the Drum*. Reno, NV: White Cliffs Media, 2000.

Gee, Judee. *Intuition: Awakening Your Inner Guide*. New York: Barnes and Noble, Inc., 1999.

Greenland, Susan Kaiser. *The Mindful Child*. New York: Free Press, 2010.

Hoffman, Janalea. *Rhythmic Medicine*. Leawood, KS: Jamillan Press, 1995.

Huyser, Anneke. *Singing Bowl Exercises for Personal Harmony.* Havelte, Holland: Binky Kok Publications, 1999.

Jim, Kahuna Harry Uhane, and Garnette Arledge. *Wise Secrets of Aloha.* San Francisco: Weiser Books, 2007.

Levitin, Daniel J. *This Is Your Brain on Music.* New York: Penguin Books, 2006.

Mottin, Don J. *Raising Your Children with Hypnosis.* Bridgeton, MO: ASC HypnoClasics, 2005.

North, Henry Ringling. *The Circus Kings: Our Ringling Family Story.* Garden City: Doubleday and Company, Inc., 1960.

Pasco, Lee. *The Magic of Make-Believe: Beyond Positive Thinking.* Scotland: Findhorn Press, 2006.

Schwartz, Andrew E. *Guided Imagery for Small Groups.* Duluth, MN: Whole Person Associates, Inc., 1995

Zimberoff, D. *Hypnotherapy Training.* Issaquah, WA: The Wellness Institute Heart Centered Therapies, 2004.